Until Nothing More Can Break

ALSO BY KATE FETHERSTON

Manthology: Poems on the Male Experience (eo-edited with Craig Crist-Evans and Roger Weingarten), University of Iowa Press, 2006

Open Book: Essays from the Postgraduate Writers' Conference (co-edited with Roger Weingarten), Cambridge Scholars Press, 2006

UNTIL NOTHING MORE CAN BREAK

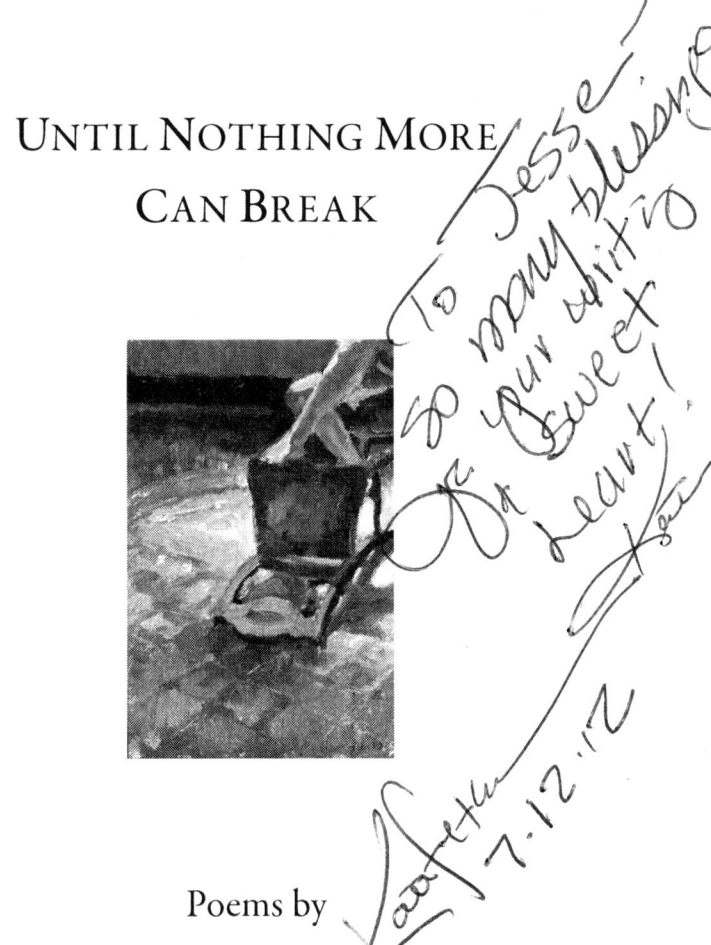

Poems by

Kate Fetherston

To Jesse—
So many blessings
on your writing
& sweet
heart!
Kate Fetherston
7.12.12

Antrim House
Simsbury, Connecticut

Copyright © 2012 by Kate Fetherston

Except for short selections reprinted for purposes of
book review, all reproduction rights are reserved.
Requests for permission to replicate should
be addressed to the publisher.

Library of Congress Control Number: 2012908843

ISBN: 978-1-936482-24-5

Printed & bound by United Graphics, Inc.

First Edition, 2012

Book Design by Rennie McQuilkin

Cover art: "Chair with legs" by David Smith
used with permission of the artist

Author Photograph by Howard Romero

Antrim House
860.217.0023
AntrimHouse@comcast.net
www.AntrimHouseBooks.com
21 Goodrich Road, Simsbury, CT 06070

For Roger

and for my parents

Acknowledgments

Grateful acknowledgment is made to the following publications in which these poems first appeared:

Artful Dodge: "Small Syllogism in the History of Love"
Cave Wall: "Albino," "Late Roses," "The Summer You Were Born"
Crying Sky: "My Block," "Spices"
Hunger Mountain: "Cooking"
Journal 88: "Lessons with the Devil"
Literary Potpourri: "Stick Season"
Manthology: Poems on the Male Experience (University of Iowa Press, 2006): "Hating"
New Ohio Review: "Saying Goodbye to Dad," "Snow"
Nimrod: "Subway," "Take Bitter for Sweet," "My Double Death as a Bowl"
North American Review: "After the War," "In the Fish Market of Praise"
Numero Cinq: "Readiness Practice"
Phoebe: "Prayer Flags"
Poemeleon: "A Bedtime Argument" (previously entitled "Inciting the Invisible to Riot"), "Setting the Muse on Fire," "Russian Rhapsody," "Balancing Act," "Ballad of Richard Parks"
Sanskrit: "Sides of the Story"
Superstition: "Fixing It," "Old Math"
Third Coast: "Blind Spot," "Taking Measure"

Special thanks to the Vermont Arts Council and Vermont Studio Center for their generous gifts of time that contributed to this collection. And to the Eat It and Hush Foundation for its support, my undying gratitude.

A debt of appreciation is due to the following friends and teachers whose help on these poems was invaluable: Nancy Eimers, Clare Rossini, Charles Harper Webb, Deborah Digges, Leslie Ullman, Bill Olsen, Robin Behn, Roger Weingarten, Bruce Weigl, and Todd Walton. To my first teachers, appreciation beyond words: Dennis Schmitz, Ron Tanaka, Julia Connor, Jody Gladding, Ralph Angel, and Richard Jackson. And to those of you whose support is the moon and stars, thank you: Ema, Terry, Ellen, Denise, Lulu, Sarah, Todd, and most of all: Roger.

Table of Contents

Prayer Flags 3

A BRIGHT AND SECRET RIVER

After the War 7
Snow 9
Balancing Act 11
Taking Measure 13
Albino 16
My Block 18
The Summer You Were Born 20
Readiness Practice 22
Ballad of Richard Parks 25
Sides of the Story: A Triptych 28
Thirteen 33
Abstract in Black and White 35
Saying Goodbye to Dad 38

UNTIL NOTHING MORE CAN BREAK

Before We Met 45
Spices 46
Small Syllogism in the History of Love 48
Cooking 50
Lessons with the Devil 52
Penelope in the Promised Land 54
Subway 56
Bowling Alley of Desire 57
Russian Rhapsody 59
Setting the Muse on Fire: A Romance 61
Stick Season 63
Red Purse 64

In the Fish Market of Praise	66
Late Roses	68
Still Life with Autumn	69
Old Math	71
A Bedtime Argument	73
Winter Solstice Book of Hours	75
Hating	77
Blind Spot	80
Aperture	82
Fixing It	84
My Double Death as a Bowl	86
Take Bitter for Sweet	88

ABOUT THE AUTHOR	91
ABOUT THE BOOK	92

Time comes into it.
Say it.   Say it.

The universe is made of stories,
not of atoms.

   from "The Speed of Darkness,"
   Muriel Rukeyser

Until Nothing More Can Break

PRAYER FLAGS

The living catch and rub
each other down to reveal

not stone or gold but
subterranean water

unfurling like rags
torn from the shirt my love

wore the day we met, and braiding
the bedsheets that will rip

still warm when we part. These poor
flags strung from arterial

branches bear my broken
pledge to honor what I can't

keep and what I can't tear
away. Note the cracked cup with its restless

lip-mark gathering dust by the phone. Through
vertigo between hello

and goodbye, I hum tenderly while
polishing our alabaster

bowls with scraps of indigo
and my own fine hair. Finally

every story spills out as emergence or
emergency depending

on one's view of the hole in the ozone
left by having a self.

A Bright and Secret River

AFTER THE WAR

Nights of my childhood, Dad, instead
of painting in your garage studio, you'd
sip a Manhattan studded with two
cocktail onions, something fancy from before

the war, when you danced on the Jersey shore
to Benny Goodman with women whose pearls
gleamed from moonlit throats. Back then,
you'd have taken the train down from New York

where you drew stylish ads for magazines, while
bread lines swelled with men who rode
boxcars looking for work. Those years, you played
tennis, sang tenor in a trio—luck and youth

on your side. On a lark, you joined the National
Guard for the polo ponies, but, sent to spy in France,
abandoned for dead on D Day, a man you didn't
recognize woke up in a hospital two years

later, who, when you could walk again, headed
west until the money ran out. There you met
my mother, a raw-boned girl young enough
to be the daughter you didn't yet

have, and angry enough to keep you both
alive. You spent my childhood hunkered,
quiet so the nightmares might
lose your address. Instead of painting,

you twisted leather strips around broken
huaraches to the sound of Mexican
ranchero music blaring from a makeshift
radio. Just a kid, I'd sneak in behind your

back and filch onions from your drink, vinegar
dripping down my chin. You'd blow
smoke rings from Chesterfield Kings, and if
you weren't in a bad mood, I'd

hang around memorizing paint cans, brushes,
gesso-lined shelves, lingering
over the color wheel, figuring who knows
whose coat of arms tacked to drywall, sawdust

scattered on cool cement. I hoarded these
scraps as if attention to detail could
lure you away from grief, as if in the right
light you could come back. I kept asking who

the blonde was in that painting you did years
before I was born—she swayed on a bent
nail by the screen door, glowing with color
and possibility. You never would say, but

maybe you knew she was how I'd look
thirty years into a future you couldn't
bear to see except through my eyes.

SNOW

The winter I invent god, I steal the black
and white photo propped against
Mom's dresser mirror where she's
six years old, just one year younger
than me. Smiling at her father who's
outside the frame, she's showing off new
white cowboy boots. I've heard whispers
that her father only stayed alive for another
year, that then she was worse than alone
with her brothers. Later in my playhouse,
I rip the photo into shreds and bury
them under the lilac bush. For extra
luck, I squish a secret potion of pyracantha
berries over the top, wishing Dad's hands

wouldn't keep shaking even when his
blanched knuckles stop
short of Mom's fury and he shouts, "Don't
make me mad—I could kill you but
it'd be an accident—like the war when
I couldn't stop." Sometimes he plunges
a blotched face into his fists and cries.

Nights I sneak from my cold bed
and pray to the hall heater's fiery
blue eye to take me anywhere I won't
have to come back from. When I sleep,
I dream of icy ash dissolving white
into the black tangled branches

of our apple tree out back, its gouged
bones blurring under a slack-jawed
moon whose pale mouth opens
and swallows whole
continents of my ancestors
until there is only snow.

BALANCING ACT

Agile as a dancer, Dad balanced
a dictionary on his head, showing me how

to walk like a lady, which Mom
couldn't do. He swayed down the stage-

lit hallway on the balls of his feet, calling
over his shoulder, "Look, Katie, it's easy!"

From the couch, Mom, who could
slam dunk a basketball but got her

pinkie stuck in the charm
school teacups, eyed Dad—smiling but

not smiling. What did I know? I tried
to flatten my head by pressing down

hard on my skull with my chin
teetering on the windowsill at night.

I'd pray to the moon, *Make me
graceful.* I practiced faithfully, still

the book always fell. Home sick
from school, I'd steal

Dad's Allspice scented shaving
mirror and navigate the house

by ceiling. Freed from gravity, I sashayed
effortlessly around corners, a ballerina

in disguise. So, when Dad
cautioned me at dinner with, "A girl who

sings at the table will marry
a fool," I only lowered my head and kept

humming into the plate
of liver and onions.

TAKING MEASURE

If the universe is governed
by precise design, Groucho's
father the tailor paid

no heed. With his naked
eye, he believed he could gauge
a customer's measurements, which

is why he needed to continually
cultivate new precincts for practicing
his peculiar sartorial twist. Once,

instead of delivering the finished
suit, Chico pawned the pants
and his father had to buy them

back even before the customer
refused to pay. Thus the poor tailor
paid twice for his own

unwearable clothing. Would I
lie to you? Notice the new
leaves busting their lousy

winter coats, and those lilacs
elbowing out from too-tight
bruise colored buds. Sure, you

and I know it's all temporary. But
even the air steps aside for fools
and those with excessive

vision. When Mom packed
me off to the school
for the blind, shards of sunlight

broke over the heads of the other
albino children whose
white hands fluttering

over my face calculated
how close I came to being one
of them. Whatever they saw

with their fingertips, they only giggled
and flocked away. The distance, said Mom,
was too great to bear, so she

drove me home. For years, the tender
red-eyed children blinking under
a desert sun haunted my waking

and my sleep. In a tangential
absence, I grew apart from these, my
tribe, mismatched and scorned. Until

I recognized myself in you, you souls
of ordinary remorse who slip
the cock-eyed world on like a sleeve

that dangles fringed and unraveling
in the wind. For we are all the whole
history of love, which is as I see it,

a bad idea made
beautiful. And, of ideas,
my little darlings,

there are no other kinds.

ALBINO

Who can tell what is natural
from the way things are? To begin with, nothing

can be seen but an aura
of electricity. Gloves are the hands kept

folded in a cedar-lined drawer, my shock-white
hands the gloves that remain. Good reader, glimpse

my body as psychology: I'm the handmaid without
a mirror, adlibbing reflection snatched from rumor

and lies. View my body
as theology: an occasion of grace, unabashed

of syllogism—note logic's not
god's doing. Or, think of me as geography: each

vein's dendritic course striates alabaster
thigh and forearm. Notice

I disappear against sunlight, against
snow, become eyes that gaze into the soul

you don't believe in but which
you fear. You see a ravenous wolf, or your

unstrung mother, or some angel of birth and death
from a play you were supposed

to have read. You swear you're not
like me, but you can't

flee from the night where
I'm at home, where my hair is starlight

crosshatching subterranean
currents, my face the moon dipped

in bones, and where ink-dark trees
squat by the river, each

grasping for its blind twin, each
whispering, *Who is like me, who?*

MY BLOCK

Here comes the familiar terror where, one blink
and I'm a mere squirt of a kid, back at Connie Boyd's
house next door. Old piss and vegetable rot assail
my nose as Connie's mother's ingot eyes
peer helplessly into mine. She's too dumb
to ride the bus or go outside alone. Once, she
bought my mud pies encrusted with birdberries
for fifty cents, a fortune in that family. I got
the belt from Dad, and when Mom
marched me to return the money, Connie's
mother only opened her palms, smiling
and confused. Yet, even now when my heart
starts bucking, I'm lost again inside that
labyrinthine house of hers, bare save a few
sticks of broken furniture and a couple old
mattresses, where the naked windows aren't
framed by walls painted aqua or pink like
everyone else's but magenta, Indian red,
the raw pigments of a scream. And Connie's
mother gazes at me pleadingly for something
I can't give or name or escape and suddenly
I ache for my smart, angry mom, for
the look of her back at the sink, disapproving.
Or, even for Jenny Harmer's mother who
wears hairnet and curlers all day primping
for her husband who gets home at six. Jenny's dad
once shoved her mom through a plate glass window
and I wasn't allowed to play there for three whole
weeks afterwards. Or maybe I might trade

Debbie Merwin for *her* mother who lets
Debbie live on Cokes with fries
and watch horror movies all night plus
curl her hair, but who's out till the wee
hours with men not Debbie's dad. No,
anywhere but Connie's house where
Connie's father in the service drops by every
other month for a couple of hours,
where long ago the Bermuda grass
has given up to the spleen of stray dogs
and kids with matches, and where one raggy
rose spiders along the crumbly stucco,
its used Kleenex blooms the sweetest
ever, but Connie's mother can't even leave
the house to bury her nose in them. Yet, even
when I run away, my feet slapping the hot
sidewalks until I limp home,

                                      always the yelling
catapults me back to Connie's side yard
where those ugly-as-snot flowers
struggle for breath and I lie in the dirt, scabby
knees to my chest, as sunlight randomly blesses
my parched Eden, and I dream of sheltering
trees. Half a lifetime away, a full-leafed
maple overbranches my window where
I'm struck dumb with the old rootless
fear, a mute child hunched over this crummy
page when, in a flicker of light, Connie's mother
flits from her crazy cave behind my eyelids
but even so, out the open doorway a green
wind unleashes summer rain.

THE SUMMER YOU WERE BORN

Clouds lounged in Mexico City's cobalt
heaven above narrow market streets where
Mom and I walked to the *zocalo* to buy
red bananas and chilies. Six years old, I wedged
between hunched *abuelas* swathed in mantillas,
farmers slapping reluctant burros with sticks,
and kerchiefed *senoras* whose overflowing
shopping bags nearly whacked me but
Mom would hand me a fat mango, slit
with her pocket knife. Each saffron slice dripped

paradise down my chin. Afternoons, hanging
over our balcony, I sucked lungfuls of smog
ripe with dahlias and *Bolillos* baking
across the street, eager for the five o'clock storm
to short out traffic signals. Cabbies fishtailed
through the intersection cursing at businessmen in stalled
limos who'd flick cigar ashes out their windows. Everyone
in the street shouted their bets on guys in undershirts
spontaneously fist fighting in the meridian.
Then the rain would snap off like a shut faucet, traffic

lights blinked back on. I was supposed to keep an eye
on our five year old brother, but evenings I'd sneak
to the roof, daydreaming about Mount Ixtaccihuatl
doomed to be separated from her lover, her white
necklace of ice gleaming sadly through the mist
of her dress. Once, our brother climbed the stairs
on his chubby baby legs to find me and tottered
toward the roof's edge, his red jacket waving *goodbye!*

before I snatched him back. "Why
weren't you watching?" my mother scolded. Sundays,

we'd ride gondolas at Xochimilco,
Old Mexico City's canalled waterways, where
hibiscus and lilies anointed the red boats—their blind
petals read my face while I drew
words that disappeared like my breath
in the stinky water. That summer, Tom, my littlest
brother, as you were waiting
to be born, you soaked up equatorial
light lavished with the happiest
of our parents' dreams, the last of their careless
plenty. I tried to remember the colors for you
before your eyes blinked awake into the darker
world we came to call our lives, but I forgot
everything until the moment you first lifted
your newborn son—then the bright and secret
river that carried us unknowing opened its arms.

READINESS PRACTICE

Fighter jets loop fat chalk
marks on a turquoise

sky while I'm daydreaming
out my third grade

classroom window. The air raid
siren blasts and Mrs. Fisher hollers,

"Kids, get under your desks, arms
over your heads!" I crouch beneath

my pink metal bomb shelter, eyes
squeezed shut, waiting for the end. *This*

is what the last minute will be like,
I narrate to myself, *The bomb*

drops just like that, an enormoid
ball of flame bigger than the sun, but

it's like reading *The Weekly Reader* out
loud and my mind drifts. Through

the classroom's open door insects
pop and click. Weeds reeking

in desert sun: stinkweed, goat heads,
and alfalfa by the tether balls where

I practice praying to see if
it works. *Please, make Dean Posey*

love me. But he turns his buck-toothed
smile toward that nasty Cindy Mercer

and a sonic boom shakes the swings when
he asks her to play kickball. I punch

the deflated yellow ball against
its whining pole, hard, and I picture

the shrunken ball sucked away and
swallowed by a relentless

heaven. The fragile thread attaching
me to gravity

snaps and I whoosh into space,
whirl farther and farther above

this little earth, crash into John Glen
and the Cosmonauts. Cracking open

one eye, I peek at my desk's moonscape
underbelly of gum wads and dried

snot, wondering if the sky has
a ceiling like my bedroom at home

with its glow-in-the-dark stars, and maybe
you smash into it when you die, but what's

after that? Now, Mrs. Fisher's voice
slams me awake, "Children, readiness

practice is over. Your arithmetic
test is next." And, climbing back

into my seat, I smell eraser
dust. Cindy Mercer's eating paste

again; Dean Posey throws up
his baloney sandwich, and everything's

back to normal.

BALLAD OF RICHARD PARKS

By the time we're nine, she's
skinny legs under a sack
dress, but Denise's almond eyes
glint with skeptical intelligence beyond

boys' power to resist. She steals
inside her body to escape notice, but
Richard Parks begs to carry
her books and finally

she lets him and doesn't
care that he's the boy every
girl at Acoma Elementary wants
to marry. She'll blossom into

the woman hiding inside her father's
lumpy gray cardigan, trying to bust
her biological clock so the cat-calls will
stop, so she can shine from her own

light, but when we're nine, already I'm
the girl lusting for adventure. I'll tell you
where babies come from and, for ready
cash, I can enumerate the Latin

names for bodily functions that
sound so much nastier than just plain
shit. My head wrapped in jacquard
scarves and a cast-off shawl, I don't

fit anyone's idea of beautiful, squinting
behind red glasses, my thatch of white
hair held askew at a theatrical angle.
The day after I bribe Richard to play

doctor, he ignores me by the monkey
bars and later he's walking her
home and I hate her for that, but
she likes my stories and I need

an audience more than an enemy, so we're
best friends by sixth grade when Richard
and his whole family disappear overnight.
Everyone—even the teacher wringing his hands

when he tells us—loved Richard Parks. It's
Kennedy shot all over again, but never
mind. That day, our adolescence is done for, even
before Denise trudges Jackson Junior High's halls

head down, trying to ignore the leers. And even before
I'm sobbing in the girls' bathroom when pimple-ridden
dog boys won't risk talking to me and my mother
says, "But you have a beautiful soul," which is the final

blow so by now I'm speed reading novels where sallow
faced women lean artfully into loneliness and where
virginal sunlight through cracked windows
illuminates a single white bed, all tidiness

and erasure. Later, when we're twenty,
Denise waves feminist tracts in my face while
she's retreated to bib overalls and the monastic
cell of her childhood bedroom.

Meantime, I'm pacing downtown alleys all hours
in my Goodwill get-ups, a flask of Southern Comfort
tucked in for warmth. Now that we're thirty-nine,
life's the usual disaster. We're strolling the Los Altos golf

course pushing her babies, and I'm kvetching
about my lesbian divorce, when I think I see Richard
in two-tone loafers and peach polo, but it's only
some tax attorney flashing Rolex. Denise punches my arm,

cracking up, and I'm doubled over laughing as the guy
asks if we're all right. "We're just
fine," snorts Denise, grabbing my shoulder. Richard
Parks, wherever you are, you're home free.

SIDES OF THE STORY: A TRIPTYCH

My Side

Did I break Suzanne's nose on purpose?
Sure, my sixth grade heart throb Rodney
mooned after her like a sick calf, and that
could've been enough. But also that time she

invited me to spend the night at her house, when,
before dinner, Suzanne and her parents changed
into nice clothes and we sat on fancy chairs
with our legs together like ladies while

her dad made drinks: a martini with three
olives for her mom and Shirley Temples for us.
"I like to wait on my girls," he said, winking
at me. My own dad had devolved from tragically

remote to scary, so when Suzanne's father
in his navy suit and tie bent smiling to offer
me an extra cherry, I couldn't stop
wiggling in my hand-me-down corduroy

skirt. After dinner, outfitted in matching satin
robes, Suzanne and her mom chatted for two
hours rolling Suzanne's luxurious hair into pink
curlers while I watched, embarrassed by the toothy

zig-zags my mom had cut into my hair with pinking
shears. And Suzanne wore a real bra under her lacy

nightie. I'd shimmied into my Mary Poppins P.J.'s
hiding in the bathroom, praying no one would see.

Later, Suzanne's father stooped to kiss her lumpy
hairnet like she was his perfect doll. Next morning,
the radio woke us playing "Good Morning Starshine"
and we ate pancakes made from scratch. Her dad even

pecked her mom on the cheek before going to cut
the grass. I could hear him whistling as I fled
and ran all the way home where Dad
muttered, "Balls!" before disappearing

into his garage, and Mom banged
pieces of the broken washing machine
scattered all over the kitchen floor. Next day
on the playground, there was my elbow—

the tether ball swung high—there was Suzanne's
nose, and I never got invited to her house again.

Suzanne's Side

Katie remembers it all wrong. Even though she
pinned her heart on her sleeve for buck-toothed
dishrags like that Rodney, and she wore weird
red glasses, I still liked her. But something

about the way she watched my mother
roll my hair got under my skin. Why
didn't her mom do hers? And where
was her robe? Also long after we should've

been asleep, she wouldn't shut up, wanting
to know what I wanted to be when we
grew up. How could I tell her all I wanted
was to get away from my parents hovering

over me like I'm a vase about to shatter?
That I can't breathe with their
fussing, their plans for me. How could she
understand, still in her little girl pajamas when

I already had breasts. I watched Katie sleeping,
just a little lump in the next
bed. With her odd life, she had nothing
to lose, whereas I had everything—a perfectly

nice life with doting parents—and I couldn't
stand it. Also she lied about the radio
song, which was, "Raindrops Keep Falling,"
my all-time favorite, so I remember.

For courage, I'd whisper, "I never worry
when the rain keeps on falling, because
I'm free." For all her strangeness, she
was the one who could've

helped me step outside my suffocating
world, but then again, even though we
were the same age, she was just a kid.
And another thing, she didn't break

my nose. I broke hers and I'd do it again.

Suzanne's Mother's Side

I'm losing my daughter and she's only
in sixth grade. I hate those soft
curls I pin into rollers every
night. My husband's retreating

to polite solicitude. Frosting the martini
glass, he pours my drink as though
I'm the Queen of Sheba. As though I'm no
one, a stranger. He's begun insisting on dinner

dress, acting like Suzanne and I are
his dates. I warned her she's to wear
that new bra under her nightie because
you can't be too careful of men's

urges, and also you have to keep
your body while you can. Appearance
is everything, even if it doesn't
last. Who knows when you'll start

sagging, your face turn blowsy, your breath
turn vile? I bought us matching
robes, dotted with pink roses like my
high school prom corsage, but that

night, after too many doubles, I imagined
how I'd place the pillow over Suzanne's petal
perfect face. I'd lean into my husband's
arms while I arranged baby-pale buds

on her casket. Stumbling into Suzanne's
room, I yanked her awake, hugged her
too hard, then crawled into my cold bed.
That girl Katie never stirred. My husband

is having an affair. He can't stand
the confusion, everything
changing, our daughter's star rising, our
oblivion. Suzanne's already a woman and I'm

a middle aged drunk. Who
will love her and how will he
fail her? I forgot there's a breakfast
guest. I'll slice strawberries, blood-

sweet and steeped in mint. I'll whip
up French pancakes and cream.

I hate my life.

THIRTEEN

That summer my big brother
stole my diary. He circled the parts

about him in red ink, as if I'd made
a mistake, but I hadn't where I'd said

he tried to tongue kiss me which
was gross and disgusting, although

not the final insult. I kept
pounding out my words like little

soldiers risking their lives
for me. Yet I lugged my brother

around inside like a copper necklace
that stained my neck green. I'd hear him

puffing outside my door, scheming
how he'd snatch the pages. What

did he really want? At last I shoved
my ten-pound Royal typewriter

under the bed. Writing
was too heavy. I vowed to be more

considerate of others. But every
human face I knew,

I hated. Those I despised scribbled
invisible corrections on my

naked wrists: *you ungrateful
girl—you have made this story*

*ugly and we will not
forgive you.* At night, the moon

skinny dipped in a verdigris
sky, and sang only

to me. Out of nothing, I made
this poem and whispered

breath into each word. From whoever
tried to break it, I hid its beating

throat between my cupped
hands. Afterwards, my brother

turned good. I bled a little
but I didn't die.

ABSTRACT IN BLACK AND WHITE

For a whole year, I didn't speak and no one
spoke to me. Every day I rode the bus
downtown where smart white girls didn't
last. Drunks not quite passed out held
court in pawn shop doorways, swapping
furry-lipped mumbles, grabbing

air as my hippie skirts flapped this way
and that in the hopeless wind. Age-worn
women at the bus stop weighted down
with unsootheable babies sidestepped
dust devils that stung my ankles
with beer tabs and empty food

stamp booklets. Inside Kresge's dime
store the lights looked warm so I'd
wander overstuffed aisles of plastic
notions listing dangerously above
the rutted century old floor. Everything
marked down, nothing sold. The boy I loved

loved another
boy. The dad I loved
hated and loved me, hating
himself. My best friend pretended
to study theater but
refused to leave her room. Swaddled

like a swami, she read
constantly, pausing only to whisper

invective. I skipped college classes
to sew gauzy get-ups from found
remnants but never remembered
underwear. Nights I'd gorge

chocolate alone in my basement
apartment, then pace alleys courting
trouble. So, I startled when, one bitter
afternoon outside the dime store, a sweet
faced boy touched my arm and said, "You
remind me of Agnes Martin. You know,

the painter." I looked around, wondering who
he was talking to. "No, you—with your white
blonde hair—you're an angel, too elemental
for mundane reality." I shrugged but didn't
turn away as he squinted at the gray smudged
horizon and intoned, "Agnes Martin's black

and white paintings reveal an abstract
dialogue that speaks to the spiritual
dilemma of our time." What
was he talking about? I couldn't imagine
heaven—I was lonely enough
on earth. From a backpack, he unwrapped

smeared Xeroxes like some Torah—Martin's
crisscrossed black lines scurried
over blank backgrounds with a draftsman's
frenzied attempt to get out of jail
free. Suddenly, the dirty cloud cover
cracked open and I envied

sunlight breaking like fresh
egg yolks over his hair. For the split
second his eyes met mine, I glimpsed
the woman I could become. "Give
me your address and I'll send
you her stuff," he grinned, waving

goodbye. Decades later, this morning's
paper says the painter's dead. I still
don't know anything
about Agnes Martin, but my best
friend from all those years ago
calls and we kibbitz about cooking, while

outside a goldfinch trills
its delirious song.

SAYING GOODBYE TO DAD

My dad died alone in a VA hospital
as July sun beat without mercy into the raw

seesaw of breath busting seams between
each cell. *Third spacing* doctors call it

when cell walls no longer sustain
boundaries with integrity, fluid

sluices into interstitial no-man's
land and overpowers whatever little

plans were made for a garden and some
trees. When my brothers and I got

the news and flew in from the various
places to which we'd fled, I'd just split

on my first lover after years of her
threatened suicide, bouts of drunken

depression, and refusals to take
her meds too numerous

to recount. Her view: I'd been trained
strictly for fixer-uppers, too stupid

or stubborn to leave, but, waxing
romantic, she'd croon, "You'll do me

for a rough old mate." The day she smashed
my stuff into the carpet and poured

ten pounds of flour over
everything, I might have stayed for

more of the same, but I threw
crumpled clothing into my pack,

startled when she whispered, "I'm
just like your crazy

old man, aren't I?" I didn't
answer because we both knew

how I'd cried into my fists, waving
goodbye to my dad for what

I thought was the last
time while he'd punched air

screaming, "You're nothing but
a fucking cunt just like your

mother." I'd have liked to say
it was just cancer corroding good

intentions, but those had derailed
years ago, driven off the edge

behind gallon jugs of Dago
Red at lunch followed by conga

lines of Manhattans with Librium
chasers meant to numb the shrapnel

knifing throughout his body
and the yelling, the cold

shoulder he and Mom passed
back and forth. On visits after

their divorce, I'd watch Dad berate
juncos through a one-way

window installed for privacy. Next,
he'd offer a Coke, then time to go.

But once, clouds heavy with
summer rain, he beckoned me

outside and recited names
of plants used to living with thirst:

piñon, prickly pear, yucca. Casually,
back turned, Dad said, "You'll be

a writer, kid." For a moment
he seemed almost happy, then

we got back to being silently
at odds. "But there were good

times, weren't there?" he blurted
through sobs, after cancer

kicked in. To my shame, I said
nothing. So my brothers and I

returned to find our dad no more
present than a calculation of flat

New Mexico light hammering a beat-
up arroyo. In lieu of a memorial

service, my brother Tom and I
stumbled noon-blind into a fake

Spanish-style stucco, where
a sallow boy, tripping on his

papa's suit cuffs, mumbled
condolences, his tongue at a loss

in a mouth of bad teeth. "Let's get
the fuck out of here." Tom gunned

Dad's car past vacant lots where
exhausted junipers squatted in sad

shadows, taking it up on two
wheels by Roosevelt Park, our

childhood oasis, now just bent
cottonwoods on pee-spotted

Bermuda grass. "Come on, floor it," I egged
Tom on, picturing Dad's ghost seeing

red. "This'll get him," Tom choked as he
jumped a curb and skidded into the parking

lot of that novelty shop where we
scored a rubber chicken and red fuzzy

dice for Dad's rear view. Tom hollered
out his rolled down window, swerving

over double yellow lines until we hit
mesa dirt where the sun bled

naked into our backs, spending its last
on sagebrush and coyote bones. By nightfall

Dad's car ran out of gas. Stars poked
holes in the sky over Sandia mountain

and into the front seat where we sat—
gourd-hollow, gutted, lost.

Until Nothing More Can Break

BEFORE WE MET

From across the room, you scorched
the air between us like formaldehyde

dizzying me back to that
summer I conjugated New Testament

Greek from 3x5 index cards taped
to a stainless steel autoclave while

soaping blood from speculums and
dilators. Carefully I tied nets of half

formed embryos into blue plastic
containers and ladled a few

teaspoons of formalin over each sac before
sealing the jar. "In arche ain ho logos," I mouthed,

In the Beginning was the Word, while
the radio played one love song after

another. I stacked, weighed, and measured, then
burned what seared its secret language into

my fingernails, my hair and skin, into the stopped
up hollow of my throat. That's how I knew you

before we met. That's how I carried
what was lost

before you opened me.

SPICES

Who was the woman waiting by this same kitchen
window for her love as I watch for mine? Bare
branched now, the apple trees on the hill were still

green when I arrived. She'd already gone, leaving behind
drawers of tea towels, cupboards stocked with sticky
tins, a blue hooked mat by the tub as if

she'd be back any day soon. As September turned,
I mourned the last of her irises as they sank
into autumn weeds. Now that winter's coming,

I climb her rickety pantry ladder, reach the highest
cupboard, and peel away the taped yellow recipe
for Ginger Fig Confection, along with a moldy

list of common household poisons and their
antidotes. I pry each spice loose, inhale their stale
grass or spring dirt, then smooth down new

red flowered paper and arrange my jars
of saffron and sage that carry light from a house
on the other side of the country, from seasons of use

and loving before I loved this man who reads
at the table while I chop carrots and leeks for soup.
Sleeping next to him at night, I caress the fine hair

that novas at the small of his back, breathing in
the cedar of him against my cheek. Sometimes
when moonlight slants through our bedroom, I lie

awake counting hydrangeas on wallpaper she
hung long ago and I wonder how
the years to come will work their beautiful

ruin. Tonight, after sweeping up, I'll walk
outside and pour the spent spices beneath
pines bent with snow.

SMALL SYLLOGISM IN THE HISTORY OF LOVE

Because a man asks to share
her piano bench when both
are late for the lecture, it must

be stated there's nowhere else
to sit. As Q surely follows P, ice
bangs against the window

like an animal begging to be
let in. And because she and the man
dive into a *sotto voce* of illicit

nonsense, the white and black
keys vibrate coiled halftones
behind them. His voice

mocks and teases; thus she
imagines a bear tossing
its head, admiring

a honey tree and she
closes her eyes when
he laughs. One gene more

or less and the universe
unravels on its axis like a rubber
ball disgorging

guts of string. Therefore, my
dears, it constitutes a necessary
condition that the last

thing to go before death finally
unmoors us is this urge
to weave blankets of memory

and to rub their salt
stained nub into our souls.
Even so, there's no telling

what kind of trouble
might lie ahead as his
restless fingers shuttle

sparks which arc
above her breastbone. Still,
as the lecture drones

to a close, the inevitable
concludes and she
whispers a single word into

the lobe of his inclined
ear because god
first spoke through burning.

COOKING

When my friend calls to ask
if I'll be her husband's

second wife should the tests
come back positive, I'm cutting

up shallots and ginger for another
soup my love's kids

won't like, crunch the phone
to my ear and keep

chopping, even though she's
crying, "He can't

be alone—I know that. And you'd
be good to my kids." Outside my window

sun picks through mountains
wadded like laundry someone's

left in the hall. Spring
won't come. I won't find

work. The kids reminisce
about dinners their real

mom cooked better. The forecast
is freezing rain and all kinds

of ice. My friend says, "I know
you're living with that guy—I

would understand if
you couldn't." But I stir

in barley and kale
and I see our ghosts

rising with the steam where
one woman passes her life

on to another who
stands at the stove, waiting.

LESSONS WITH THE DEVIL

Tea in a cinder-block
room on an unmade
bed. A cigarette carton careens

against the whiskey
bottles on a shelf. Through an open
window, summer voices

lull and buzz. I stumble over
my tongue, stammer envious
admiration for his seductive

linguistic genius, when
I realize the devil isn't
listening. He interrupts, wonders if

I can see his aura—which I can but
it isn't shiny. The top of his head merely
melts into blank walls as he strokes

his beard, confiding, "To become
a poet takes as long as it takes water
to discover and to forgive

itself." I'm digesting this
alchemy when the devil, warming
to my audience, warns of certain

tendencies toward transcendence
that are premature and out
of sync in my work. Later, while

we walk outside, he fishes a corkscrew
from his pocket, flips it into the air,
and gets to his own

agenda: "That man
you're sneaking around with
isn't for you—he's bad

news—I should know. Besides,
I could make you
other offers." The devil snaps

his fingers and the corkscrew
flashes. Pewter clouds eclipse
the sun. I wait for a brimstone

symphony, for night to bludgeon
my already bruised heart, for the devil
to say something that will finish

me off. But light streaks back
out of glowering nimbus
and the grass is green

again, and, when he turns, he's
just a man and we
go on walking like that.

PENELOPE IN THE PROMISED LAND

Now that my neighbor's unspooled
from the bobbin of her memory, someone
must watch her. This morning, I drag

kitchen chairs to the window where sun
refracts our reflections, hers and mine, in
crazy quilt patterns. I arrange a frayed

jacket around her shoulders while we
gaze out at mountains snoozing beneath
a late winter snow that blows

off the roof and dazzles mid-air. She
leans close, murmurs, "There
it is: lightfall." Our breaths smudge

and disappear on the glass. Silent, I don't
speak of my mirror brimming
with demons. I don't mention the sleepless

fear tangled in my throat when
the man I love turns from me
in the night. Her head gyrates

in sync with brown wrens darting
by the woodpile. To shift her attention,
I speak up, "Look how snow comes after

all that can't be done." She unravels
blue threads from her jacket's elbow
and dangles them to the tilted

farmhouse floor, as if to say, *You dull,*
stupid girl! Love always comes to this,
but never mind. I gather the strands

in cupped hands but she's
no longer waiting for anyone to return
from some odyssey. She's intent on that

early robin stabbing at grass stubs through
snowmelt, fixing us with its black
eye. Water pulses from the pecked

weeds, the same water changing from
cloud to breath, traveling backward
to the sea. "Oh!" She suddenly grabs

my arm with a sinewy hand. "Something's
coming. I know you know!"
And even though I don't, somehow I do.

SUBWAY

This morning the subway's nearly empty, but
an ancient woman inside a mountain of rags
squats by the tracks shouting curses

at voices in her head, or at us, or the dead—who
can tell. We're still being careful after yesterday's
squabble ended with our making love like paper

boats struggling against undertow. Just up the tracks
a dreadlocked guy intones a two-chord
autobiography, guitar case open for cash, while

an opera poster for *Aida* salutes his tragic
composition. A few silent graybeards in black
overcoats line concrete benches, waiting as if

for news of rain or some other
reason to go on. The train's late, but no one
except us is going anywhere. You turn,

head pointed away, but your body heat
pulses to mine. What will I do on the day
that you board one train, and I

another? Even when this crooked heart
shall vanish, love, my ashes will sing
the shimmering music of your name.

BOWLING ALLEY OF DESIRE

That last Thursday night
at the Cardinal Lanes, I was just
one of the regulars

from the other
side of town. Del Paso
Boulevard's blue neon streetlights

backlit the bowling
alley bar where, on the counter,
pickled eggs swam in red

juices. A Bud Lite sign spat above
racks of stinky shoes. It meant
nothing that my love

turned away as she pulled
off her coat and leaned to light
a cigarette, that she smiled

at someone else's joke. It meant
nothing, but when I blinked, somehow
I lost her. And now, thousands of nights

and miles away, sweet man, is our
love less terrible? This morning
you pull me toward you as dawn

edges around the blinds. I slide your
cock into my mouth, your face
unreadable in the half light, but

I make out your tender mouth
forming its exhalation. Your tang
on my lips, your hands in my hair—

and still I see her framed in the 40-watt
flicker of the old bowling alley, how she
bent low, and taking her chances,

rocked a cranker down
the dim lane where it gathered
speed, and guttered.

RUSSIAN RHAPSODY

"You weren't really a lesbian," my love invoked
one morning from beneath a mound of blankets
just this side of bliss. Oh, wasn't I? Ok, the first
lover: crazy and I didn't love her, so it doesn't

count. But the second I did and because she
loved me back, I could love you, dear man. This
I felt impelled to clarify between gasps as we inched
a Viennese grand piano, its Carpathian walnut

groaning, up our steep hill in subzero February
while stars shattered the frigid heavens
above our private Siberia. Hours and days
we shoved and nudged. The new millennium

unscrolled backward along frost-bent
apple trees that guarded a snowlit
meridian line of black ice until
the burnished beast crawled inside

our woodcutter's cottage, creaking its relief
as he rested his hand on the carved
candle stand. I eased bone-chilled
sharps and flats into a Russian rhapsody

under the gold sway of lamplight where
my love's hair, in a murder
of question marks, exclaimed halleluiah
and his face beamed like the last

great Hebraic physician to the Czar.
"You weren't really cold out there,"
I nuzzled him later. "You just lacked
a working knowledge of what

warm could be. That, bubbala,
is where *I* come in."

SETTING THE MUSE ON FIRE: A ROMANCE

I'm lying face up in traffic, asphalt digging
into my tush, head fuzzy, when
an 18-wheeler swerves, barely missing
my phantom pink pedicure. Just as I spy the muse
punching the Walk sign, he shouts in my direction,
"Enough with the drama!"

"Who do you think you are," I shout back,
easing onto skinned elbows. "Where
have you been anyway? Out on medical
leave? Scamming Social Security?"

"You're getting the two of us mixed up," he snaps.
"I'm not some 900 number fantasy you call up
and dump after you've wrung out one of those soppy
tropes you're calling poems."

"Those are odes to natural beauty and my higher self," I sniff.

"Bullshit," he growls, "What a crock! Nature's
up to its eyeballs in pus and the religious
right along with your higher
colonic! You just want a cheap
vacation—well, don't
plan on using me to get out of your
crummy dog-eat-dog world."

"Woof woof, fuckstick," I spit back, "Your
self-esteem's catapulted off the monkey
bars at the peek-a-boo stage. If no one

chased you around the desk anymore, you'd
be blaming the Internet and my left
nipple for your disappearance from
the lexicon. So cut the high and mighty, boychik.
You need me."

"Oh, all right," he concedes, and helps me up
with a grudging grin. "How about you lose
that tatty number you're sporting and we crawl
between my sheets with a couple of beefsteak
tomatoes, a Ouiji board, and a match."

STICK SEASON

What of my body, primed
for small tenderness, its seasons
of blood coming to an end? If

only I could spring
as lightning to the edge
of a storm-lit meadow, I'd gather

a chorus of thunder at my back,
and into that magnetic heaven, I'd howl
the names of those I love—yes—and

those I longed to love. But each
syllable would tumble to the sullen
earth, immutable as November rains

rotting haystacks and shucked stalks
of corn. Now it's stick season, when
tamaracks don their goodbye

gold and naked maples poke up
beside muddy paddocks, strike
reckless freeze frames in a game

of red light, green light. And the voices
of my children hover
unborn in the chilling air, their bodies'

husks splintering each moon into stars.

RED PURSE

In the hospital waiting room's cheap
Vermeer print, a woman reads a letter, while
air suspends itself in pale

wings above the fine print that enters
her with a private fire. Burnishing
inside my right breast, a tiny jeweled

fist with no direct address uncurls finger
by fibrous finger. Cloistered with the other
women in backless robes, I overhear

one whisper to her friend of the pelvic
mass, the unexplained cell
division, her voice a dull serrated

blade cutting through daytime TV. Next, I'm
a Tandoori mannequin on my back in rare
antiquities where the ultrasound

technician's professional digits spotlight
my inner accessories—this abraded geography
of pearls so secret, even you have not

taken them into your mouth, even you
have not traded their weight with your
knowing hands. Later from under

the bed sheets, you murmur, "Tomorrow
I'll buy you that smart red purse. I'll waltz
you around the world in a glimmering

sheath only I can see through." I lie
burning in your arms, while above
our lunar landscape, gauze-white

curtains exhale the drunken
angels who see into shadow with eyes
of shadow. Speechless, they wait

for someone to bear their blistering
voices into the blood-marked
body of this world.

IN THE FISH MARKET OF PRAISE

In the fish market of praise, a woman will be told
her price. Measure her. Weigh her bones that will not

cleave to one another, but which beckon, flee,
unravel. All day she drinks rosewater,

mint, and orange to perfume her innermost
juices. But what will she wear

to her bat mitzvah? She is our little sister
who has no face. Her skeleton unpetals,

eludes X-ray. The body's clarion resonance
judges poetry redundant. Poesy courts the body

passionately, and yet with whimsy, sarcasm—yes—
all the pretty stops pulled out of the organ

grinder's waltzing mouth. So what if there's no
language for grief? Stuttering is the best

any of us can do. But our little sister has no
tongue. What shall we do for her on the day

she shall be spoken for by the lonely
seeker of pearls? Stumbling, her mermaid tail

flops below the sack-drab dress her mother
chose for this occasion. Blue-green scales drop

like scabs onto the pavement. Rhinestones adorn
her ears and nose, a jewel pierces each lip. Flashes

marking the holy openings. With clary sage
and sandalwood she anoints each palm, while

blindfolded waiters mambo between
illegally parked cars bearing gilded trays

for the ring of gawkers: starfruit, lox and bagels, good
Shiraz. But she is a woman who riots

against the grasp of granite and schist, who
extrudes geodesic heat that fractures her fragile

shell. Our little sister who has no breasts
harangues the boundless ocean until

only the moon can love her. If she be a wall,
we will build upon her a palace of silver.

If she be a door, we shall enfold her with cedar.
And should she crumble, we will scatter her

dust as spices by the sea, for to gravity
she remains herself alone, and she is lovely.

LATE ROSES

At first light, a taste of something darkening,
a belly smell sweet and hot, the shards

of some dream I can't recall, but as I wake
I open the window where watered

sun pours over late
roses, and I inhale a bittersweet tang

from childhood—when I ate
petals of verbena, carnation, honeysuckle, rose—

all the flowers of my mother's desperate
garden, one by one I tore them

and sucked the scents into my mouth. Now, the last
autumn flowers push their sex up into the dim air,

red and magenta tongues poised
like clangers of unrung bells

about to speak, about to spring away.

STILL LIFE WITH AUTUMN

Alone in our bed, I woke at half
light to geese crying their urgent

goodbyes. Now, this late October morning
sears the screen door through which your last

saffron tomatoes sway; the sunlit globes
swagger even as they dangle from shriveled

stems. Our ginger cat sits in the windowsill,
intent on a woodchuck foraging up the apple-

littered hill. Her spring-green eyes track
that furry appetite with teeth scuttling

into meadow grass beyond white
roses I planted for the moon and for

the shadow of the moon. By now, they
should be dead, but blossoms keep unfolding

as they haven't all summer, luminous buds threaded
and caught in deer netting I'd set out to save

July's lilies. Lazy gardener! Now the lilies
nod their old heads downward, ochre

stalks relinquishing fixed
beauty. The cat's tail conducts

a silent orchestra in time to maple
leaves twisting free, five-pointed

universes finding and losing
purchase. There is

no still life. Even stars incite
the invisible to riot between

each mote of dust. Though tomorrow
you'll return, you will be changed,

as music spills out its heart, as even
my life does not belong to me.

OLD MATH

Little zeroes of shrimp hide in my Pad Thai
as I lean on tired elbows at the Royal

Orchid Restaurant pretending not to listen
to my love's friend Zeb complaining

how, when he retires, his wife will make him
move to Flatbush. And my dear one, warming

to the subject, offers, "Yeah, remember when
that ex of mine sent me back into the three alarm

fire for her slides?" Of course, Zeb does, so he says,
"How about that babe, when she

was done with you, ending up with your
brass knocker collection?" While they trade

damage reports, I count lotus flowers triangulating
on the tablecloth and remember that long ago

dinner date who'd nudged Father Knows Best
glasses up his nose, explaining he'd bought

my paintings because all he had was a rented
TV and a bed. He'd figured by now some

woman would've maxed his credit
cards on kitsch then dumped him, so

he was surprised to find himself
alone in a near empty house

with cash to burn. A pair of cheap candles
dimmed as his blue cardigan slalomed

toward my side of the table but his eyes
snapped like a junkyard dog when I

reached for the check. He spat, "I believe
in the old math where men

pay for everything." In the bone
marrow accounted between that

night and this, I've sustained
my own losses. Who can calculate

reparation? I can't count that high without
falling asleep. Suddenly I'm back at the Royal

Orchid where, dead quiet, the men's
feral eyes pin me, glinting,

accusing. "For Chrissake, you two,
give it a rest." I load a fork of curry

for each of them—"Taste this;
there's plenty."

A BEDTIME ARGUMENT

If insomniac excitement was what you craved, why
didn't you hook up with an acrobat you could keep
plumped with a bicycle pump? Go ahead—

pout behind that newspaper, bone up
on how Chinese authorities inoculated
fourteen billion chickens—anything rather

than engage your sweetheart apropos
the gallbladder attack visited upon our
bliss. You blame philosophy. "Sophism's

a narcoleptic, not an aphrodisiac," you kvetch.
Ok, I admit my urge to unravel
the meaning of internal objects begs a swift

karma sutric boot in the pants, but when
Wittgenstein says in the case of a miracle we must
imagine god—don't your short hairs twizzle

in the cosmic breeze of my
direction? My wondrous darling—all
I want is an answering

seriousness. Ah, but glance
my way and I'll shape-shift—*shazam!*—into
the torque-defying trapeze artist you

dream of who'll nibble your paradigm
shift down to bare pixels
of pleasure. Yet, since the last

paragraph of that mystery novel you insist
on tucking under your pillow reads
"Oh Beulah," he breathed, rummaging

*in his pocket for the pearl handled straight
razor, "it's always been you…"* I'm a bit
leery of falling asleep first—

know what I mean?

WINTER SOLSTICE BOOK OF HOURS

After the fight, he says, "I did the best
I could." Instead of, "I'm sorry." Though she

isn't accusing. She's moved on, that's what
she tells herself. *What the hell,* she thinks. As Marilyn

Monroe said, *What the hell is always
an appropriate response.* A chicory blossom

sky, senselessly out of season. He reads
the paper's pet section aloud: *Rats Want Home.*

She wonders what he's telling her, squinting in case
she can decipher the code: "It's all ones and zeroes,

right?" She imagines the rodents' hungry
bodies huddled blind, suckling

the old cat. Dusk now. The window admits
cool lavender. Outside, river shadows pull

loose gold threads to holes. Other mistakes
blow in too, ghost

guests at this, the last table of the longest
night. She nips cooking wine

straight from the bottle. *For my
cold,* she thinks. *Every beginning disturbs*

the end. Darkness weaves a precise
silence along the fine hair of her arms.

Tipsy, she confabulates book
and Bible, murmurs to the snoozing

cat, *We are lilies, you and I. Though utterly
lost in a dark*

wood, we neither toil nor spin. She dozes,
wandering a haze of black

and white rats scuttling through tender
snow. Oh, look! Above the icy

roof, aloft those slouching
trees! Arbitrary as birth, a new

year's dumpling cheeks dimple
the indigo-hatted moon. She barely

wakes as he untucks the blanket
and shifts the cat just enough

to curl in beside her.

HATING

Tonight's howler blinds
the windows and our bedroom lights

stutter on and off but, sweetheart, your
back barely betrays the play of muscle

and breath as you bend over rows
of ties. Your bastard father who

never read you spilling black
blood across a blank page—news of his

death's a biblical scam where, having
sacrificed his first born, he must've

thought he could extort from the Most
High a perpetual low golf score and that economic

waters would part forever in his favor. Now he's
no doubt surprised to be suspended

somewhere in the firmament like the high
wire bridge you gunned in that maroon

'63 Impala he gave you instead
of a birthright. Just a boy, you screeched

out of town lit up on righteous
fury, but couldn't stop

scanning your side mirror for the father
who was busy trying to forget

your mother pulling away from the curb
on business of her own—the only

deal he ever lost. You've smelted
your heartbreak into a life without

regrets, lived
outside even the radar

screen of his contempt, but
late in the cataclysm of near

fatal surgeries and midnight
phone calls, I hid in the hall

eavesdropping while
you stammered on the line, your

voice breaking as I cursed
his impoverished

god. *Good riddance to bad
blood,* I spat into my clenched

fists. So, now you slide
your hands through 40's silks, Italian

geometrics, a garish
print from the kids, and, turning,

hold out a blue
shadow asking, "Is this

good?" My heart lurches
like a trapeze artist arching

backward off the wire. The net
disappears at your

gaze, my love—how you ravage
me with his

beautiful goddamned eyes.

BLIND SPOT

On screen Hitler's secretary, Trude Jorge
smokes herself into oblivion, sporting
a colorful scarf to hide

the tracheotomy. Blue movie light
pinpricks your silver hair on the periphery
of my vision. My thick rose

glasses glint with a merry go round
world out of focus, shapes
reeling wherever I glance. Only

darkness stands still. From my childhood
window, indigo sky crouched
on black haunches, its one

white eye trained on sullen
ranch houses, asphalt, gravel
gardens. In my wedding night dream, another

man's ghost hunted me down
muck-stained streets until
I turned and gouged out his thieving

eyes. Hitler's secretary, Trude Jorge, waited
fifty years to spill her
memories of the Fuhrer's distaste

for anything erotic, the endless
flatulence only his dog
could love. Last February when

a woman my age jumped
into the Rio Grande Gorge, she left behind
the milk crate she'd used to climb

over the guardrail onto the ledge. The river,
a thousand feet below, ran
high with snowmelt. Believing she

could fly, she told friends she'd send
postcards from Milwaukee. Trude Jorge,
aged twenty-two, rode in the Fuhrer's

train with its blacked out
windows to the Berghoff, where
she lived locked until

Hitler left them all
like that. She didn't
know, she said, ready now

to ask forgiveness for her
blind spot. So, tonight you
read me the jumper's

story, and I ask if you believe
in god. You shrug, "Who
can believe every

single day? Come, lie down
with me." Lamplight drizzles
honey over the curves

of your hands. And even
the silence between us
loves us recklessly.

APERTURE

One molecule away from chlorophyll, my blood
thrums to solstice light. Elderberries sweep

flute-limbed branches across this dirt
road where a monarch zigzags

drunkenly through Queen Anne's
lace, surprised to be evicted from its

chrysalis. Once, a cedar twig
fell from heaven and I

subsisted on that idea of green
from one moon's open

eye to its dark neglect. Born with no
mouth, the Luna moth's seven day

life is all sex; its still and unwavering
desire basks in high summer sun.

Up the road, already purple flowering
raspberries shyly blossom while nectar-

throated columbine shrivel to seed.
What absentminded sage or benign

idiot said, *When your foot touches
the ocean floor, then waves of yes and no*

disappear. Another year, a whisper
of saffron nourished me through the fallow

seasons. Thus, my mouth is not
my mouth, my body not

my body, but a star-flowering root's
secret about

a secret. Hollow and awake, this
trembling air: my one life.

FIXING IT

One hundred winters ago, a horse huddled
beneath this carriage house in a fieldstone
and earthen pen waiting for hay
forked through floorboards, snorting
and stamping for summer heat's
prickle along its back.

I am bent to a wheel I cannot see.

The carriage house lists now against a ragged
breathwork of clay and frost heaves. A ghost horse
still whinnies under our uneasy
car and we agree the structure needs
a fix. You tear out rotten floorboards, layers
of poverty and make-do: tar paper, carpet, weight-
bearing beams supported by nothing.

I cannot bear this weight. I rest on nothing.

This morning you find a nest of midnight
bees homing between crumbling stone and old
cement. "Sorry," you say, "they
have to go." The danger of swarming, the nearness
of death.

A blind moon squeezes my heart open and shut.

Up the hill, I'm ripping weeds from lilies when
you poke your head out from the work
below, a halo of black

buzzing in your hair. Laughing, you call, "These
bees are gentle—they can stay." You shake
your head and the fat
wizards lift into wind, drift into my open
throated peonies.

Each bee in its life makes but a teaspoon of honey.

Lazy and pleased, they keep their insect counsel
as you prance like a boy in June's green sun.
Floating somewhere in the air, I lean on my shovel
and watch until you disappear.

Enough by god, and nothing more.

MY DOUBLE DEATH AS A BOWL

When I die, I'll come back as a bowl and squat
proudly on the kitchen table, my painted

innards a beauty to behold. No way will I
be salt and pepper shakers perennially begging

to serve. And certainly not candlesticks lit
for disappointing holiday dinners. I won't

return as a vegetable knife, or kebob
skewer—I detest pointing anywhere. Luxurious

on my ceramic back, I'll stretch out empty,
and press my two faces into the gleaming

moment between moments that pass
slowly. Some days, I might roll an orange

at my navel to say, "Looky here!" Other days,
I'll close my glazed eye and dream of light

so pure my heart might splinter into
a calligraphy of cracks that

you'll finger absently wondering if I'm still
worth keeping. But then you'll lift me, admiring

my handmade imperfections, and place
me on a windowsill where you remember

and also forget. One day, chasing squirrel
shadows, the cat springs and I

tip and shatter. You sweep the shards, sad
at how fragile everything is, how nothing

lasts, even me. Until we are both broken,
until nothing more can break, until then.

TAKE BITTER FOR SWEET

Each poem a stranger shanghais us sleep
drunk into a rickshaw rattling through this small

town dawn—incongruous
and alone with only our strangeness

for company. Yes, and under a sea of stars we fall
backward into our lives, from water

into water. I, half-witted insomniac, outside
in my robe at first light, attempt any negligible

truth, but, as usual, I'm not
equal to the task. Bleary, I stumble

into the honeysuckle bush whose silver leaves
cup orange and crimson berries. I measure

the weight of fruit in my hands, each
destiny held by nothing. Call it gravity, chance,

or family dynamics by whose impeccable
vertigo we navigate constellations drawn

from a game of pick-up sticks. Still,
the dust of the world is everywhere, luminous

as this air I'm breathing while upstairs in our bed
you're softly snoring. Your unhappiness

blossoms over our pillows, its runnels
whisper my helplessness. All I have

to offer is a handful of alizarin, plus a few
liquid notes from the finches shacking up in our

neglected apple tree. I say neglected, but
what I mean is, left to wildness and the love

I will surely die of. If every poem's a stranger,
then this dark form leans

against ghost light while a rickety
travois clattering

down an unlit street spills the loose
beads of my need

for you. The paperboy tosses today's bad
news at the neighbor's porch, as I

mingle my breath with yours, same
world, same cast of fools and angels

taking bitter for sweet. Isaiah the prophet
preached, *Woe to those who mistake*

gall for honey, day
for night, but my tongue

fills with brine and rose, apple
and ash, when I say life's

hard enough—let us make of it
what we can. This exile

calls you home.

Kate Fetherston's poems and essays have appeared in numerous journals, including *North American Review, Hunger Mountain, Nimrod,* and *Third Coast.* Co-editor of *Manthology: Poems on the Male Experience* (University of Iowa Press) and *Open Book: Essays from the Postgraduate Writers' Conference* (Cambridge Scholars Press), she has received several Pushcart nominations and was a finalist for the Pablo Neruda Prize in 2008 and 2010. A psychotherapist in private practice in Montpelier, Vermont, she holds an MFA from Vermont College. This is her first collection of poems.

This book is set in Garamond Premier Pro, which had its genesis in 1988 when type-designer Robert Slimbach visited the Plantin-Moretus Museum in Antwerp, Belgium, to study its collection of Claude Garamond's metal punches and typefaces. During the mid-fifteen hundreds, Garamond—a Parisian punch-cutter—produced a refined array of book types that combined an unprecedented degree of balance and elegance, for centuries standing as the pinnacle of beauty and practicality in type-founding. Slimbach has created an entirely new interpretation based on Garamond's designs and on comparable italics cut by Robert Granjon, Garamond's contemporary.

To order additional copies of this book
or other Antrim House titles, contact the publisher at

Antrim House
21 Goodrich Rd., Simsbury, CT 06070
860.217.0023, AntrimHouse@comcast.net
or the house website (www.AntrimHouseBooks.com).

•

On the house website
in addition to information on books
you will find sample poems, upcoming events,
and a "seminar room" featuring supplemental biography,
notes, images, poems, reviews, and
writing suggestions.